D0719065

70001438641 4

Dough Craft
IN A WEEKEND

Dough Craft

IN A WEEKEND

More than 50 stylish designs to make and decorate

M O I R A   N E A L

NEW HOLLAND

To my mum,
Sheila Robertson,
whose enthusiasm, creativity
and zest for life has been my
greatest inspiration.

First Published in the UK in 1996 by
New Holland (Publishers) Ltd
24 Nutford Place, London W1H 6DQ

ISBN 1 85368 728 6 (hbk)
ISBN 1 85368 729 4 (pbk)

Editor: Emma Callery
Designer: Peter Crump
Photographer: Shona Wood

Editorial Direction: Yvonne McFarlane

Reproduction by Hirt and Carter (Pty) Ltd
Printed and bound by Times Offset (M) Sdn. Bhd.

Acknowledgement Now that the months of staring stupidly at
the computer are over, I would like to thank my daughter
Claire for taking over the typing after she had found I had
spent 887 minutes to type 5,437 words. I do not think word
processing is my forte. To Gareth, who in turn, nearly wore out
the stair carpet as he repeatedly had to come up to my rescue as
words vanished from the screen. (Thankfully, he had predicted
my inadequacy and had made three copies!) I would also like to
thank Sally for the use of her Aga when the fan oven situation
reached crisis point, and Tony for not filing for divorce!

I particularly want to thank Lynda, whose enthusiasm,
support and help I shall never be able to repay and my mum for
her endless cups of tea and dog walking. Thanks also to Daler-
Rowney for supplying artist's materials, and Lakeland Plastics
and Bostic for their assistance.

Important: In the recipes, use either metric or imperial
measurements, but never a combination of the two, as exact
conversions are not always possible. Every effort has been
made to present clear and accurate instructions. Therefore, the
author and publishers can accept no liability for any injury,
illness or damage which may inadvertently be caused to
the user whilst following these instructions.

CONTENTS

INTRODUCTION

Who would believe that a visit to the library for a book on creative writing could start an obsession with salt dough modelling? I walked in and there it was. A brand new book on the subject. I decided that I would give it a go and by the next day I had made my first creation: a bowl edged with fruit which was much admired.

Needless to say, the creative writing disappeared in a cloud of flour; dough had made a take-over bid for my time and kitchen. Never again was the oven cool or the kitchen clean. I was in the stranglehold of this compulsive hobby. Even while the dinner was cooking I'd quickly mix a batch of dough and rustle up a new and unique object.

Soon, I had read all there was to read on the subject but felt hungry for more. Not a day passed without an experiment into a new method of basket weaving, vegetable design, pencil top or light pull. I concluded that anything can be made from it — and, indeed, that it just what I have done; shelf upon shelf of dough-made items. I think that the moment of truth finally arrived in the supermarket the day I had seven bags of salt in my trolley and the cashier enquired if I was expecting bad weather. It then occurred to me that we, the salt dough fraternity, have seriously distorted the figures that the boffins produce about our annual consumption of basic commodities like flour and salt. Do they realise that so much is being converted into works of art (or indeed missiles should anyone dare say anything uncomplimentary about them) not body fat? Ah well… we know something they don't know!

As for dough craft being the ideal weekend pastime, well — all you need to do is delve into the depths of your kitchen cupboard for flour, salt and cooking oil, mix the lot together and you are instantly free to explore the world of modelling. Likewise, many of the modelling tools required are to be found in a kitchen drawer so you don't need to spend many days planning in advance.

Many of the ideas included in this book are extremely quick to make: a few twists of salt dough sausages here and some deft modelling of small apples and blackberries there and you instantly have a twisted autumn garland. Of course, the overnight cooking is something that can't be rushed, but once the dough is dried out, the painting and varnishing for the finishing touches really don't take many minutes. So, with modelling on a Saturday and painting on a Sunday, here is the ideal weekend activity. I hope that you get as much fun out of it as I have and whether you are already a hardened fanatic, or just starting out, there should be enough ideas in this book to fuel your enthusiasm. I need an excuse to write another!

Moira Neal

GETTING STARTED

The basic ingredients for making the dough and then modelling it are few and easily obtainable. This is what makes the craft so appealing - almost everything you need can be found in the kitchen, and most other items in the garden.

YOU WILL NEED

Apron	Polyurethane varnish
Plain flour	Drill
Cooking salt	Florist's stub wire for hanging projects: thicker gauge wire for large projects (wire coat hangers are ideal for this), paper clips for hanging smaller models
Large mixing bowl	
Weighing scales or measuring cups	
Wooden spoon	
Small container of water	Wire cutters
Baking sheets	Pliers
Lard for greasing trays	Two-part epoxy resin or hot glue gun
Aluminium foil for covering nonstick trays and for supporting dough while it is being cooked	Craft glue
Dredger	
Rolling pin	**USEFUL BUT NOT ESSENTIAL**
Unserrated knife	
Fork with even prongs	Biscuit cutters (handy for making refrigerator magnets and small decorations)
Old pencil	
Grater	Brooch backs, magnets and earring findings if you wish to make refrigerator magnets and jewellery
Card for templates	
Scissors	
Set of circular cutters or a selection of empty cans and bottle tops	Cake icing cutters (these really speed up production and quickly pay for themselves)
Cocktail sticks (toothpicks) for indenting, texturing and supporting	Cardboard roll for napkin rings
Garlic press for hair, grass and roots	Clip frames
Drinking straws for coring out holes	Clock movement
Black peppercorns (wonderful for eyes)	Modelling tools
Cloves	Nylon icing bag and nozzles
Few twigs for stalks	Potato ricer for simulating rag doll hair and willow
Paints	Small piece of nylon netting for making texture
Paintbrushes	

If you do not have a good selection of baking trays and dishes, take a few trips to your local car boot or jumble sale. It always pays to fill the oven each time you make dough. If you want to make picture frames, buy old frames and use the glass, and you can also pick up mirrors of all sizes which can easily be converted into works of art.

ADDITIONS FROM NATURE
It is always fun to have an excuse to go for a walk or take a trip to the seaside and salt dough provides one. The autumn is the time to collect beech nut cases, fir cones of all sizes and seed heads. Also make a collection of twigs to be used for stalks in place of cloves if you wish. A beach walk will provide shells (make sure they are empty first), tumbled glass, driftwood, stones and seaweed, all of which can be wetted and pushed into the dough. Old nuts left over from Christmas also make unusual additions and the cracked outer shells of pistachio nuts make wonderful mouse ears! If you have a bowl of pot pourri, you may well find an interesting collection of tropical seed heads and cones that may also be used.

MAKING SALT DOUGH
The following ingredients make one batch of dough, as refered to in the projects in this book. Use weighing scales or a set of cup measures.

270 g (2 level cups) plain flour
320 g (1 level cup) cooking salt
180 ml (¾ cup) water
10 ml (2 tsp) cooking oil (optional)

1 Measure the dry ingredients. If you are using cups, fill each cup to the top and levelling it off with a knife. Take care not to pack down the ingredients.

2 Mix the ingredients together and then add the water, again filling the measure right to the top. Bind the ingredients together, turn out onto a work surface and knead for 10 minutes. (A food mixer with a dough hook is ideal for this and really helps to produce a good workable dough.) It is important to knead the dough for the full 10 minutes as it develops the gluten content and makes the dough easier to work with. To check that it is ready, roll a small amount into a ball and it should not crack. It should also feel firm and slightly tacky. Add more water very gradually if needed.

3 If you find that you need much more water than the quantity stipulated here, change to a different brand of flour. Too much water makes the dough less workable and it takes longer to cook. Once you have found a make of flour and salt that work well for you, stick to them and you will find it easier to get consistently good results.

4 Some people advocate the use of cooking oil and wallpaper paste in their dough but the above dough should work very well without the oil added. If, however, you find the dough difficult to work, add the cooking oil; it will help prevent the dough from sticking to your hands and is recommended if you are working with children.

COLOURING DOUGH

This is a great technique for those who do not like painting and is ideal for children as the only finishing needed is two coats of varnish. Food colours are ideal for this purpose when light fastness is not a problem, and may be added either as the dough is being made or kneaded in afterwards. If a complete batch is to be coloured, dissolve the colour in the water before adding to the

dry ingredients. Use liquid paints or gouache for a more light fast finish. Mix them in by taking small quantities of the dough. Roll them out flat, add a little colour in the middle, fold over and then knead the dough until the colour is evenly distributed throughout ①.

It is also possible to use natural ingredients to colour dough, and coffee (dissolve first in a spot of boiling water), cocoa, paprika and spices are all ideal ②. Hang the finished model out of direct sunlight for longer-lasting

colour. For a variety of colours, make up the dough first and then divide and colour as required and keep each colour in a separate bag.

Alternatively, for a rustic effect, use a selection of different flours. In this book, buckwheat has been used for some of the leaves on the natural dough wreath (see pages 44-5) together with rye flour for a paler effect. The doughs were made in the same way as basic dough, but substituting the chosen flour for the plain flour. More or less water may be needed to get the consistency right and, as buckwheat flour is gluten free, it is quite fragile to work with. The made-up dough for both buckwheat and rye will keep for weeks stored in an airtight container.

PREPARING BAKING TRAYS

Lightly grease baking trays with lard to ensure the safe removal of your model. Non-stick trays tend to mark the back of the dough and so it is worth covering them with aluminium foil first.

TIPS FOR SUCCESS

• Always knead your dough for at least ten minutes.

• Keep ready-made dough covered and use within a few hours of making for the best results. It starts to become floppy as the salt dissolves and may be unmanageable by the next day. It is possible to reknead for ten minutes with the addition of more flour, but for the effort involved, it is as well to start from scratch.

• Stick dough together using water, either with a small paintbrush, or use your finger. Avoid wetting the surface of dough which is not to be painted as it will mark during baking. Any nuts, twigs or other bits you are adding to your model should be wet before positioning. Should they come loose during baking, secure with glue once the model has cooled. You may prefer to make up a little dough paste to use as a gluing agent if your dough is slightly dry, and this is done by adding water, a little at a time until you have achieved a mushy consistency.

• If you have dough left over at the end of a project why not rustle up some of the small ideas shown in this book which you can use to fill the spaces on your baking tray? Alternatively, make some spare leaves, fruits and flowers to practise painting on.

• If you have a really large project in mind, measure the internal dimensions of your oven (avoiding the back to allow free air circulation) and buy or have made a suitable sized baking sheet; sides are not required remember. I have found that aluminium is the best metal for baking on.

• Bake dough as soon as you have finished modelling it. If it is left to air dry first, the surface becomes crumbly and any unsupported leaves tend to break off easily. When dough is baked in the oven a chemical change takes place which strengthens the finished model.

MODELLING TECHNIQUES

The key thing to know about salt dough is that when you are sticking anything together, whether it be strips for basket weave, or fruit and vegetables to decorate, you should always use water. It acts just like glue.

TEXTURING SALT DOUGH

All manner of household items can be used for printing texture and it is worth building up a collection of buttons, pieces of lace, wood and cake icing embossing tools. The more you look around, the more ideas you will have.

Use scissors to make a fur or feather effect. For fur, make tiny snips into the dough varying the angle all the time. For feathers, make even rows of V-snips following the natural line of feathers. This method can also be used for texturing trees, making hedgehog spines, and for making ears of wheat ①.

To give a woolly texture, grate the dough. Then carefully pick up the grated dough using tweezers and place on the wet dough model ②. This gives a fragile finish, but it is fine for a wall decoration which is not going to be disturbed.

MAKING BASKET WEAVES

There are a great number of possibilities here but the simplest effect comes from using a fork. Choose one with even, equally spaced prongs and use regular pressure as you push it into the dough. There are three variations shown below ①.

Alternatively, start with a rolled slab of dough and then apply strips of rope. Work in one direction first and then the other ②. The Italian-style basket of fruit in the plaques gallery (see pages 26-7) has been decorated in this way.

To make a coarser, woven wood style of weave, again start with a slab of dough and cover it with strips of thinly rolled dough, weaving them together as you stick them to the base ③.

MAKING A TRELLIS

A trellis can either be made using a lattice pie cutter (such as some of the baskets in the gallery on pages 36-7), or for a more freehand feel, stick together strips of dough, working first in one direction diagonally, and then everlapping the stripes in the other ①.

PIPING DOUGH

One of the most exciting aspects of using salt dough is experimenting with new modelling techniques. Piping is a quick and very creative way to model salt dough and a nylon piping bag is the best thing to use as it holds a lot of dough and is re-usable. Among its other uses, use piping for adding features to faces, tendrils to ivy, and writing names and messages. It is also useful as a glue to stick larger pieces together and the consistency can be altered accordingly.

To make the dough a suitable consistency for piping, take a small quantity of dough and mix with water until it is mushy. You may need to experiment to get a pipeable consistency. If required, add food colouring or gouache paints at this stage (see page 9). Place a piping nozzle (nos 2 or 3) in a nylon piping bag, add the dough and treat as icing.

Similar effects can be achieved using a clay gun and with its large number of discs other effects may also be found, but you will probably not need to add any more water to the dough.

MAKING HAIR

A garlic press is useful for making hair as well as vegetable roots and any length may be obtained by opening the press and reloading with dough. A sieve or fine netting may also be used for making fine strands.

A potato ricer is another interesting gadget to use with the dough. Put a small quantity of dough in at a time, cover with a piece of baking parchment and squeeze. Refill the ricer until the dough is the right length. The parchment will enable you to open the ricer more easily. Riced dough makes wonderful rag doll style hair and can also be used to make willow wreaths and garlands.

MAKING A DOUGH ROPE
If you were a whiz with modelling dough when you were little, making a smooth, even rope will come easily to you, but others may find it surprisingly difficult. The dough must be very well kneaded to make a successful rope. Roll the dough lightly using your fingers but if you have trouble making a smooth rope, roll with a baking tray instead of your hands.

To make a twisted rope, make two identical lengths and lay one rope diagonally across the other. Starting in the centre, work towards one end, alternately flipping one piece over the other. Repeat for the other end ①. Do not try to twist both ropes together as this causes tension and the dough will split. Cut the rope to the length you want and wet the ends to hold it in place.

MAKING A PLAITED ROPE
Start with three, evenly thick sausages of dough. Stick them together at one end with a little water and then lay the right-hand rope over the middle one to become the central rope ①. Do the same with the rope on the left, taking it over to the middle ②. Keeping the tension even as you work, repeat until you have the required length. A plaited rope looks equally pretty if it is worked in three different colours.

MAKING UNCUT EDGES
In my early experiments with napkin rings, I rolled the dough into a flat sheet and then cut out strips of dough. However, a cut edge can look very untidy and so, to make neat edges for napkin rings and flat basket weave, for example, try this method.

Roll out a sausage of dough and use a rolling pin to flatten to the desired width and length ①. This results in an uncut edge that is far neater than cutting the dough with a knife. It is best to avoid using extra flour for rolling out if possible as it tends to dry the dough and cause the edges to crack.

MAKING TEMPLATES
There are several ways of making templates. For a simple outline, either use the templates given at the back of this book (see pages 76-8) or draw your own on cardboard. To transfer the outlines on pages 76-8, trace over the appropriate shape using tracing paper and a pencil. Then draw over the outline on the back of the paper, position it on the cardboard and go over the top one more time. Cut out the resulting shape and use this by laying it on rolled out dough and cutting around the edge ①. Remember, though, that some of the most natural looking leaves are those that are cut freehand using a sharp, pointed knife.

Alternatively, draw around fresh leaves to make cardboard patterns ②. Or make your own, re-usable, patterns by drawing around or photocopying the leaves and then sticking the outline to some cardboard and cutting out ③.

MAKING NAPKIN RINGS

Many of the ideas in this book can be adapted to make napkin rings which are a simple and attractive way to finish off a table setting. Before making the ring itself, cover a cardboard roll with aluminium foil and then roll out strips of dough, fold around the roll and stick the ends together with some water ①. Decorate as appropriate.

MAKING FRUITS & BERRIES

Here is a selection of fruits to start you off but you will soon find you are experimenting with others. As there are many different ways of forming fruits, use the following instructions as a guide to get you started.

• **APPLES** Roll a ball to the required size. Push a blunted pencil into the top and insert a piece of twig for the stalk. If the bottom of the apple will be seen, mark the bottom by using a modelling tool. Finish with a clove ①. If you do not have a modelling tool, use a Phillips screwdriver, a drill countersinking bit or mark with a cocktail stick.

• **BANANAS** Take a piece of dough the same size as you would for an apple and roll to the required length. Use a knife to flatten the roll so that it has four or five sides and then elongate the top. Form the bottom of the banana and roughen the end using a cocktail stick ②. These bananas look best when made into bunches of three or five joined at the top.

• **BLACKBERRIES** Roll a ball about the size of a large pea and make a large number of tiny balls the size of a glass head pin. Wet the tiny balls and cover the surface of the berry. Add a calyx and stalk if you wish ③.

• **GRAPES** Make dozens of small balls of dough first and then pick them up in your hands, add a few drops of water to help them stick and then 'pour' them in place ④. If the grapes are to be left unpainted, carefully stick each one in place so that they do not stain during baking. Cut a leaf and scrunch it up on the top of the bunch. Finish off with a twig stalk ⑤.

• **KIWI FRUITS** Start with a ball of dough rolled into an oval. Wet the surface and then cover it with garlic-pressed dough cut off in minute lengths to give a woolly effect ⑥.

• **KUMQUATS** Make an oval ball to the required size and then roll it over the finest part of a cheese grater to give a realistic texture. Mark the bottom of each kumquat with a modelling tool and insert a wet clove ⑦.

• **LEMONS** These are formed from balls of dough which are rolled into shape and then textured all over with each lemon with a fine grater. A clove is pushed into one end ⑧.

• **LOGANBERRIES** Make as for blackberries, but start with a cone shape rather than the blackberry's ball. Cover the cone with the small balls, starting at the tip of the cone and working towards the wider end.

• **ORANGES** These are larger versions of a kumquat, but spherical. Make as for kumquats, above.

• **PEACHES** Make a ball from the same size piece as you would for an apple. Use the back of a knife to slightly indent one side. Make a smooth indentation for the top with a blunt pencil or modelling tool ⑨.

• **PEARS** These are also the same proportion as apples. Start by making a ball and then use one finger to roll one end thinner. Push a wet twig in the top and indent the bottom and finish off with a clove ⑩.

• **PLUMS** Take a piece of dough about half the size required for an apple. Roll to an oval. Use the back of a knife to indent one side ⑪.

• **POMEGRANATES** Make these from a ball of dough that is elongated at one end to form a crown. Push a pencil into the top to hollow it out and then snip carefully V-shapes out of this and fan out ⑫.

• **STRAWBERRIES** Make a small ball of dough and then roll into a cone shape using one finger. Take a cocktail stick (toothpick) and mark the pips by gently pressing it into the dough at an angle. Make a calyx by using a commercial cutter or use one of the calyx templates on page 78. Wet it and then press into place using a smooth modelling tool. This will make the tips of the calyx stand up and therefore quite fragile. Stick them down onto the berry if you prefer. Add a tiny stalk made from dough ⑬.

13

MAKING VEGETABLES & SEEDS

There are far too many vegetables to show you all of them here, but these basic ones will give you a start. Try also making peppers, onions, parsnips, corn-on-the-cob and runner beans.

• **ACORNS** Take a small piece of dough and roll it into a ball and then elongate it to make an acorn. Next, take a slightly smaller piece of dough, roll into a ball and then cup in the palm of your hand using one finger. Wet the cup and mould it around the acorn ①. Use a cheese grater to make the suitable texture on the cup. Add a twig stalk ②.

• **BRUSSELS SPROUTS** Start with a tiny ball of dough and build up layers of leaves on it by cutting out circles of dough using a 2 cm (¾ in) cutter or bottle top. Vein these either by imprinting with a real leaf or use a knife (see page 16) and apply to the ball overlapping each one slightly. Continue to the required size ③.

• **BUTTON MUSHROOMS** Take a small ball of dough and cup it in your hand using a finger. Roll out a length of dough for stalks if you are making several and cut into short pieces. Wet the cup and mould around the stalk ④.

• **CARROTS** Roll a ball of dough into a conical shape and then make several small, shallow indentations around the carrot using the back of a knife ⑤. Indent the top, too. Then make carrot tops by rolling out a thin length of dough and cutting it up into five pieces of roughly equal length. Wet these and push into the top of the carrot ⑥.

• **CAULIFLOWER FLORETS** Start off with a small ball of dough and elongate part of it to make a short, stumpy stalk with a flattened end ⑦. Press the head into fine netting to give it some suitably cauliflower-like texture, and then use the back of a knife to mark stalks ⑧.

• **LEEKS** Leeks are made from several layers and so begin by making a central 6 mm (¼ in) sausage of dough about 2.5-5 cm (1-2 in) shorter than the finished leek. Roll out an oblong of dough thinly and wrap the central core in this ⑩. The next sheet should be slightly wider. Wrap the leek so that this time the seam is on the opposite side to the first. Repeat with as many layers as you wish. Fan out the top. Pinch in the bottom and make roots by pressing a small ball of dough through a garlic press. Cut off and attach ⑪.

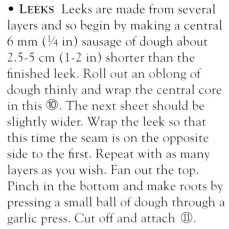

• **SEED PODS** Roll out a ball of dough into an oval shape, wet the surface and fill with dozens of small balls to represent seeds. Close the pod up slightly and nip the ends together ⑬.

• **TOMATOES** Make a ball. Cut out a calyx either freehand or using one of the calyx templates on page 78, wet the back of it and press onto the tomato with a pointed tool or blunt pencil. Add a dough stalk if you wish ⑭.

• **PEAPODS** Cut an oval of dough the length of the required pod. Form several small peas and place along the length of the pod. Damp the sides and pinch up around the peas. Add a small calyx and dough stalk ⑫.

MAKING LEAVES & PETALS

You can spend as much as you like on commercial cutters and there are a huge number on the market for the cake icing trade. You will learn by trial and error how thick to make them so that they do not break. As a general rule, any leaf which overlaps a basket or garland and is unsupported should be 3–6 mm (⅛–¼ in) thick.

Basic leaves can be made using a circular cutter. If you don't have any, start collecting tins of various sizes ranging from tomato purée to tuna fish: they make excellent cutters, but make sure you use a tin opener that doesn't remove the top of the tin as the edges can then be dangerously sharp. For very small leaves, a bottle top is ideal.

First cut out the circle and then cut into it again to make a leaf shape ①. The length and width may be varied as much as you require at this stage.

For lilac leaves, start with a circle,

indent the top of each leaf with the end of a paintbrush ② and pinch the other end to make a point ③. Mark the leaf veins using the back of a knife ④, a commercial leaf veiner or, better still, a fresh leaf. When attaching the leaves to their base, give each one a slight twist as they then look far more natural. For variations in leaf shape see Making Templates on page 78.

• **MAKING ROSES** Roses are a very popular adornment for salt dough models. They can be made in various sizes and painted all sorts of colours — just like the real thing. Start by rolling a small cone of dough to form the centre of the flower. Then cut out several petals using either a cutter or one of the templates on page 78 (depending on how large you wish your

rose to be). Using water to keep the petals in place, first fold one around the central cone, and then another making sure that you overlap the first petal on both sides ⑤. Then take three petals, overlap them and fold around the central petals ⑥. Repeat with five petals in the same way, gently fanning out each one to make a gloriously full and blousy rose ⑦.

BAKING DOUGH

It is important to bake your dough as soon as your model is complete to prevent the edges from drying out. This will ensure that your models are strong. However, as oven temperatures vary enormously, a certain am ount of experimenting is needed to find what works well in your oven. The general rule is not to hurry it. A sudden blast of hot air will cause trapped air to expand and spoil your work. On the other hand, too cool a drying process means that the chemical change needed to bond the ingredients does not take place and the model will be very fragile.

FAN OVENS

As fan ovens cook faster and tend to be hotter than convection ovens, start cooking at 80 °C (175 °F). As a rule, I cook all my dough overnight and only the thinnest items are dry by morning. All items must be baked until solid. Test by trying to stick in a pin: it will be impossible once hard. Alternatively, turn your model over and check the back for dryness, pressing behind the thickest part. There should be no 'give' at all. If there is, remove the model from the baking tray, place it on a cooling rack and continue cooking.

If you wish to speed up the baking process after about 12 hours, gradually increase the temperature to 130 °C (250 °F) by raising the temperature 10 °C (25 °F) at a time every 20-30 minutes until the model is dry. Very large models will bake quickly at this temperature. Be warned though — the dough will darken with the increase in temperature but you can use this to your advantage should you want it to appear more golden ①. When dry, turn off the oven and leave your dough to cool down slowly.

CONVECTION OVENS

Start cooking at 100 °C (210 °F) and continue until solid, or increase the temperature as above, adding 10-20 °C (25-50 °F) degrees to the temperatures.

GAS OVENS

Gas has a high moisture content which is ideal for cooking salt dough as it

allows the inside to dry far more quickly. As a result, however, there is a higher risk of the dough rising or cracking early in the drying process. So the following method is recommended to prevent this from happening.

For the first hour, cook at Gas mark ¼ with the door open. Prick any air bubbles which appear during this time with a pin. For the next hour, leave the door half open, and finally close it and continue cooking until the model is thoroughly dried. Make sure that any young children (and pets!) are well out of the way if using a gas oven with the door open.

MICROWAVES

This is a wonderful way of cooking salt dough and achieving very quick results although it is more likely to bubble up than with conventional cooking so it needs careful monitoring. It is particularly good when making dough with impatient children who want to see instant results.

Place the dough models — remember not to add anything metallic to your design if you are going to cook it in this way — on a plate (no grease required). Set the oven on defrost or the lowest setting and cook for five minutes at a time. Between cooking sessions, open

the door to allow any steam to escape; leave for a few minutes and repeat. When the model is almost dry, reduce the length of cooking time and monitor progress very carefully. As with everything cooked in the microwave, experimentation is necessary and the cooking times will vary depending on the weight of dough being cooked. A small piece of jewellery, for example, will take up to 20 minutes to cook in this way.

AIR DRYING

I have made several attempts to air dry dough but have found that the models dried in this way are extremely fragile and so I would only recommend it for repairing broken, varnished dough. Remake the broken part and then lay the dough in a warm, dry place where the air can circulate, until the dough has hardened.

⚠ SAFETY NOTE
Never rebake a repaired varnished model as the fumes given off may be toxic and flammable.

PAINTING

This is the one thing that gives many students a problem. I include myself in this as I found it very difficult to get over the 'I can't paint' barrier. Well, you can with practice. The best way to start is to make a few extra leaves, fruits, vegetables, and so on, and bake these alongside your masterpieces. Practise painting on the spare leaves and fruits, and once you feel you are good enough, progress to your models. Decide what effect you want from your painting. You may decide to paint with solid colour for a simple rustic effect or you may prefer to build up the colour for a more natural appearance.

WHICH PAINTS?

There are a number of paints on the market which can be used for salt dough, but why not start by using paints you may already have? Water colours give a lovely translucent and rustic appearance, and poster paints may also be used for a slightly denser effect. For leaves, try using a light wash of sap green and the add a little brown to darken the centre of the leaf. For blossoms use a pale colour on the edge and deeper in the centre ①. Apples look particularly good if first painted with a wash of yellow ochre. Then dry brush a little orange on one side and finish with some alizarin crimson to give a stripy effect. Alizarin crimson and black mixed together look very good on blackberries ②.

• **GOUACHE PAINTS** Gouache is a dense form of water colour and these are very useful for getting a solid covering. I like to use red gouache for painting strawberries and holly berries and they can be very effective used in conjunction with any other water-based paints. The density of gouache paints can be very useful. For example, my first attempt at painting the cat on page 24 was to make him a tabby cat, but as my painting was so bad I decided to change him to a smart black cat ③.

• **ACRYLIC HOBBY PAINTS** These come in a wide variety of colours and are very fast drying. As they are made with a base of PVA glue, make sure that brushes are washed out carefully immediately after use as they cannot be salvaged once dry. Remove any splashes from clothing straight away.

• **ENAMEL PAINTS** Enamel paints are an expensive alternative and unsuitable for children to use as they are difficult to remove from clothing. They are also solvent-based so use in a well-ventilated room. Brushes must be cleaned using thinners. Aerosol varnish should be used as the solvent in varnish will cause the colours to run if you are using a brush.

• **GOLD AND SILVER PAINTS** As long as they are either gouache or acrylic paints, gold and silver can be used before baking, but enamel should be used afterwards. Enamel gold and silver gives a really bright finish, but gold and

silver poster paints tend to be affected by the salt, and turn green! I recently tried to add glitter to some dough Christmas decorations before baking, with the same result. So add glue and glitter after varnishing.

VARNISHING

Before varnishing, allow models to dry for 24 hours — or speed up the process with a hair dryer on its lowest setting. Due to the high salt content in the dough, it will quickly absorb moisture if not sealed. This is done by using at least two coats of clear polyurethane varnish or lacquer. As there are a large number of varnishes on the market, it is best to try two or three to get the effect you want. Generally speaking, if the varnish is High Build, or feels thick when shaken, you will need to apply fewer coats than some other makes. You may find that the varnish darkens and thickens near the end of the tin and in this case, keep it for varnishing the backs of your models and buy fresh varnish for the fronts. Both matt and gloss varnish may be used to seal the dough and may even be used on the same item. For example, you may wish to use matt for a tree trunk and gloss for the leaves.

Varnish the back first by placing your model upside down on a pillow to prevent damage to any delicate surface decoration. Protect the pillow by covering it with an old sheet of unprinted plastic (the inside of a carrier bag is ideal) or silicone paper. Leave to dry for about four hours between coats and at least 12 hours before varnishing the front. Check that varnish has not run through and spoilt the front between coats.

Clean the brush with white spirit between varnishes and when you have finished varnishing, wipe the brush on a paper towel and then clean thoroughly in white spirit.

• Tip: Buy your own brush. No one can then blame you for letting it go crusty!

HANGING DOUGH MODELS

There are various ways of hanging dough models. On small pieces, a bent piece of stub wire may be pushed into the model while it is still damp. Alternatively, use a hair pin or a paper clip, both of which are coated and will not rust. If you prefer to hang with ribbon, make a hole in the dough using a drinking straw to remove a neat core.

On larger items it is best to think about hanging once they are dry. Fixing wire in the back is the best as a good hanging angle can be achieved, it is strong and also invisible. Turn the model over and support on a pillow. Using a very fine drill, make two holes in which to glue wire with either two-part epoxy resin or hot glue. On really large items, glue screw-in eyes in place

and connect with picture wire for maximum support. Door name plates may be held in place with double-sided sticky pads.

The most important thing to tell any recipient of your dough is to hang it in a dry atmosphere and it will last indefinitely. The danger time for dough is late autumn and winter when unheated porches, cloakrooms and hallways are subject to becoming damp.

⚠️

SAFETY NOTE

Never hang salt dough above a bed or within reach of a child's cot in case it should break unexpectedly. This can happen very occasionally for no apparent reason. Neither should you give dough items to young children to play with — and always make sure that any model that looks good enough to eat is well out of their reach.

TROUBLESHOOTING

• **BREAKAGES** These happen with frustrating frequency, particularly when you first start! Overhanging leaves are especially vulnerable but it is possible to salvage them using a solvent glue or, better still, a two-part epoxy resin or hot glue for an even stronger bond. Be very careful to wipe away any excess glue on the surface as water soluble paints will not cover it.

Alternatively, it is sometimes better to paint the model and any broken pieces first, then glue later. Badly broken parts may be reformed with fresh dough and left to air dry (see page 17), or be re-baked if the dough has not been varnished. This method is surprisingly successful.

• **BUBBLING** Many a work of art has been spoilt by being baked too quickly causing trapped air to rise. Poor or insufficient kneading can also be to blame. Try to make flat areas with fresh, unused dough and roll it out just once if possible. Flour, used for rolling, can get trapped in the dough in layers and cause a puff pastry effect. So if you have to start again, re-knead the dough very thoroughly.

• **CRACKS** Cracks may appear at any time during baking or during the following hours or weeks, and large, flat areas of dough seem to be the most vulnerable. Always use the minimum quantity of water to get a workable dough and avoid stretching it when transferring to the baking tray.

If cracks do appear, allow them to fully develop for several days before repairing with softened fresh dough and re-baking. If you are planning a dense coat of paint, ready-made plaster filler is a really good way of mending cracks and it sets hard within hours. The filler can then be sanded to give it a good, neat finish.

• **DOUGH BECOMES SOFT** This is due to the high salt content which allows the dough to absorb moisture from the atmosphere. If a model should become soft, place it in an airing cupboard or above a radiator until it hardens again and then revarnish and hang in a dry place.

WALL PLAQUES

This is a good starting point for dough craft. It is probably worth beginning by making a simple fruit-filled basket as this teaches you how to create a basket weave, make a twisted rope for the handle and also to make one or more fruits or vegetables. Do not worry too much about proportions when you first begin, just have fun. When I first started making dough, I made endless little baskets from brooch size upwards, some filled with little flowers for an Easter tree decoration, others with every fruit imaginable. They can be adapted to suit any occasion and be as much or as little work to make as you wish.

VEGETABLE BASKET

This makes a perfect decoration for the kitchen, or gift for a keen gardener. Substitute different vegetables if you wish and do not be put off by the basket weave. You can always make a trug shape or use one of the simpler basket methods shown in the Getting Started section (see page 10). You could also add a handle if you wish.

1 Roll out the dough to a thickness of 6 mm (¼ in), cut around the template and lay the basket on the greased tray. Use the back of the knife to carefully mark the top edge of the basket.

YOU WILL NEED

2 batches of dough (page 8)
Rolling pin
Basket template (page 76)
Ruler
Knife
Baking tray, lightly greased
Container of water
Leaf cutter or template (page 78)
Old pencil
Calyx cutter or template (page 78)
Garlic press or sieve
Fine netting
Paints (page 18)
Paintbrushes
Varnish (pages 18-19)
Drill, glue and wire for hanging

— VARIATIONS —

Make aubergines, red and green peppers, garlic, and onions for a Mediterranean version and hang with raffia. A basket filled with one variety of vegetables would make a good present for a local gardening show winner.

2 Start the basket weave by rolling dough into 7 mm (5/16 in) thick ropes or sausages, and place them vertically in pairs being sure to cover the top and bottom edges of the basket base. Trim the edges with the knife. Roll more sausages, as before, flatten them with the rolling pin and cut to length as you work. Wet and lay over alternate vertical ropes.

3 Make a twisted rope for the top and bottom of the basket from 8 mm (3/8 in) sausages of dough (see page 11). Lay it across the basket weave and trim at each edge to neaten

4 Cut and vein a few leaves using the cutter, template or a circular cutter (see page 78). Lay the leaves over the edge of the basket giving each one a slight twist to make them look more natural. Make a selection of vegetables (see pages 14-15) and, working from the edges in towards the centre, place most of the vegetables in clusters of one variety, overlapping to give the impression of abundance. Spread some of the vegetables in other places to distribute the colours and textures.

5 Bake immediately at about 80 °C (175 °F) (fan oven) or 100 °C (210 °F) (convection oven) for 12-18 hours, or at gas mark ¼ for 6-10 hours, or until solid (see page 17). Then paint and varnish (see pages 18-19). I painted the mushrooms with a light wash of yellow ochre, and mixed it with Payne's grey for the inside of the open caps; the carrots are cadmium red mixed with yellow and a little brown added in the ridges; the peas and leaves are sap green and the sprouts and tomato calyxes Hooker's green. Finally, I painted the leeks with white gouache mixed with emerald and the tomatoes with Mars red gouache for an intense colour. Drill and glue in wire for hanging (see page 19)

CONTENTED CAT
KEY HOLDER

Let this cuddly cat and mice look after your keys for you. I was inspired to make this as a certain member of our household can never find their keys. The cat is quite simple to make and may be painted in any colour you wish. I had great intentions to make him a tabby but found that my artistic talents were not up to it. However, the wonderful thing about using gouache or acrylic paints is that you can cover up your mistakes and start again!

1 Take about half the dough and form it into an oval blob to make the cat's body. Press it onto the tray until it measures 20 x 14 cm (8 x 5½ in). Use the heel of your hand to make an impression for the head and then form the head from a ball of dough flattened to 10 x 8.5 cm (4 x 3½ in) and place in position. To make the ears, roll dough 6 mm (¼ in) thick and cut a circle of 6.5 cm (2½ in) diameter. Cut into four and use two of the quarters to form the ears. Wet the curved edges and stick in place on the head. Support the ears with crumpled aluminium foil until the finished model has been baked.

YOU WILL NEED

2 batches of dough (page 8)
Rolling pin
Ruler
Baking tray, lightly greased
6.5 cm (2½ in) circular cutter
Container of water
Aluminium foil
Old pencil or pointed tool
Cake icing nozzle or plastic toy eyes
Cocktail stick (toothpick)
A few stamens
Knife
A few peppercorns
Pointed tool
Three 2.5 cm (1 in) cup hooks
Paints (page 18)
Paintbrushes
Varnish (pages 18-19)
Drill, glue and wire for hanging

— VARIATIONS —
Substitute a collar studded with jewels in place of the bow-tie or perhaps replace the mice with kittens.

2 Next, give your cat some features. This is the fun part as his character can be changed completely depending on how large or small his eyes are, for example, and how far apart they are. Make the eyes with the cake icing nozzle, or use plastic ones. Form his nose from dough 3 x 2.5 cm (1 ¼ x 1 in) wide x 2.5 cm (1 in) deep and make the nostrils using a pointed tool. Add the whiskers by making tiny holes with a cocktail stick (toothpick) and pushing in stamens that have had their ends removed.

3 Use the knife to mark his mouth and to indent his nose. I chose to give him a huge Cheshire Cat-like grin. Then add a bow-tie made from dough that is 6 cm (2½ in) wide and mark the creases in it with the back of the knife.

4 Make a tail for the cat that is 30 cm (12 in) long and 2.5 cm (1 in) in diameter and lay it in place as shown. Next, make three little cone-shaped mice, giving them peppercorn eyes and tiny ears formed from balls of dough. Add tails, each measuring 7.5 cm (3 in) long using the pointed tool to indent the cat tail first. Push the mice tails in place and twist into shape. Give each mouse a pair of arms, marking their fingers with the knife and then press the cup hooks into the hands, wetting them first. (If you prefer, they may be glued in later.)

5 Bake immediately at about 80 °C (175 °F) (fan oven) or 100 °C (210 °F) (convection oven) for 24-36 hours, or Gas mark ¼ for 12-18 hours, or until solid (see page 17). Then paint and varnish (see pages 18-19). I used gouache throughout: lamp black and Payne's grey and white for the mice, sap green for the eyes, permanent rose and white for the ears and mouth and Mars red for the bow-ties. Drill and glue in wire for hanging (see page 19).

WALL PLAQUES GALLERY

Lilac bowl

Although it is fairly simple to make lilac using a blossom cutter (see page 33), allow yourself plenty of time: I made the mistake of starting this plaque at 11pm and really regretted it.

Sheep chewing grass

The hill and sheep's body on this plaque are joined by the sheep's legs and then garlic-pressed dough has been applied for texture. The tiny blossoms in the grass were made with a cutter.

Strawberry basket

You can almost taste the strawberries in this simple flat basket plaque. The cloth was painted but you could substitute coloured dough squares for the cloth before baking.

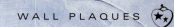

Italian-style basket of fruit

A friend suggested painting dough white to simulate Italian glazed pottery. So I sprayed the front with a few light coats of gloss enamel, and sealed the back with varnish in the usual way.

Owls on a branch

These owls were very simply applied to a thick, heart-shaped base painted dark blue. A wintry version might have cones on the branch instead of the apples.

Tropical fruits and grapes basket

Take a trip to your local fruit and vegetable store for inspiration, remembering that some fruits – such as the sliced kiwi here – look more interesting on the inside.

BASKETS AND BOWLS

Baskets and bowls can be made in a great number of sizes and are very useful for a whole range of purposes. They can be filled with home-made sweets, biscuits, cakes or perhaps with bought gifts. Or why not make a layette basket for someone with a new baby, or a needlework basket for a seamstress? I use bowls for nuts and fruits at Christmas time and pot pourri during the summer, and they are also useful on the dressing table for storing jewellery.

ROSE-EDGED BASKET

This little rose-edged basket is a perfect container for pot pourri or for serving petit fours after a summer's evening dinner party. A simpler version can be made without the handle.

There are two baking options for this basket. If you want to keep the basket empty and so would prefer not to mark the inside, bake the dish for about two hours at a low temperature after Step 1 until the surface layer is firm, and then decorate it.

However, if you intend to use it filled with pot pourri or perhaps lined with a doily, some marks on the bottom won't matter, so bake the basket after completing the decoration.

1 Roll the dough on a lightly floured work surface to a thickness of 6 mm (¼ in). Carefully lift up the dough with the rolling pin and place it into the dish, avoiding stretching which could cause the dough to split during cooking. Trim the dough about 6 mm (¼ in) in from the edge of the dish and flatten all around. To neaten the edge, make a plaited rope from three 6 mm (¼ in) ropes (see page 11) and lay around the dish making sure that the join is in the middle of one of the sides where it will be hidden by roses.

YOU WILL NEED

1 batch of dough (page 8)
Rolling pin
Oval dish with lip, lightly greased
Knife
Container of water
Cardboard
Aluminium foil
Self-adhesive tape
Rose leaf cutter or template (page 78)
Rose petal cutter or circular cutter, 2.5 cm (1 in) diameter
Calyx cutter or template (page 78)
Paints (page 18)
Paintbrushes
Varnish (pages 18–19)

— VARIATIONS —

If you do not like the idea of making a plaited edge and handle, make a twisted rope instead. You can even manage without both if you cover the edge with leaves and flowers.

2 Make a circular support for the handle from cardboard covered with lightly greased aluminium foil. Hold the cardboard together with self-adhesive tape and place it in the basket. Then make a plaited handle to match the edge and lay it over the support, pressing it securely onto the basket and trimming off the excess.

3 Cut rose leaves using the cutter or template, vein them (see page 17) and lay in place around the handle, covering up any untidy areas where the handle joins the basket. I used a leaf cutter here, and freehand leaves in the main picture opposite.

4 Form the roses (see page 17) and gently lay in place. To make the flowers appear more delicate, gently squeeze the top edge of each petal before forming the roses. For each end of the handle I made a single large rose and two smaller ones. Feel free to make as many or as few as you desire. Then add a few rose buds with calyxes to finish the whole lot off.

5 Bake immediately at about 80 °C (175 °F) (fan oven) or 100 °C (210 °F) (convection oven) for 8-12 hours, or gas mark ¼ for 4-6 hours, or until solid (see page 17). The cardboard support may be removed half way through the cooking. Then paint and varnish (see pages 18-19). I painted the roses with a light wash of alizarin crimson and the leaves with sap green mixed with a little brown.

LEMON-EDGED BOWL

Just the thing to fill with fruits or a selection of nuts, this bowl was made as part of a set which includes napkin rings, a candle holder and twisted garland. The little flowers appear blue next the yellow but were painted with a mixture of Payne's grey and white.

1 Roll two-thirds of the dough on a lightly floured work surface to a thickness of 6 mm (¼ in). Carefully lift up the dough with the rolling pin and place it carefully into the dish, avoiding stretching which could cause the dough to split during cooking.

YOU WILL NEED

1 batch of dough (page 8)
Rolling pin
Pie dish with rim, 21 cm (8½ in) diameter, lightly greased
Knife
Container of water
Leaf cutter or template (page 78)
Fine grater
Cloves
Blossom cutter or template (page 78)
Paints (page 18)
Paintbrushes
Varnish (pages 18-19)

VARIATIONS

Edge your bowl with oranges, strawberries, apples — indeed use any fruit, vegetable or flower that you care to make. If you prefer a latticework basket, line the dish with woven strips of dough (see page 10) or use a lattice pie cutter.

2 Trim the dough about 6 mm (¼ in) in from the edge of the dish and flatten all around. To neaten the edge, roll two sausages of dough 7 mm (⁵⁄₁₆ in) thick and form a twisted rope (see page 11) that is long enough to fit half way around the dish. Repeat for the other side. It is easier to make the rope in two pieces than trying to fit one length all the way around.

3 Cut out leaves using the cutter or template. Mark the veins and lay the leaves in place making sure that the joins in the rope are covered. Form lemons from elongated balls of dough (see page 13), push a clove in one end of each and place the lemons around the edge of the bowl over the groups of leaves.

4 Add a few blossoms using the blossom cutter or template. Fasten them in place with a drop of water, grouping them on the leaves and near the lemons. If you are using the cutter, stick each blossom in place as you cut them out; for blossoms cut from a template it is far easier to cut out a batch at a time.

5 Bake immediately at about 80 °C (175 °F) (fan oven) or 100 °C (210 °F) (convection oven) for 12-18 hours, or gas mark ¼ for 6-9 hours, or until solid (see page 17). Keep checking for any bubbles forming on the base during the first hour of cooking. If they appear, prick them with a pin. Then paint and varnish the bowl if you wish (see page 18) or leave the dough natural. I painted the bowl with magnolia emulsion and then used sap green mixed with a little brown for the leaves, Payne's grey and white for the flowers, and cadmium yellow for the lemons.

GRAPES TRINKET DISH

Here is a good way of using small amounts of dough which would make a very acceptable present. There are three different versions to choose from, and they are each easy to make. Why not make the matching earrings and brooch and give them to a friend?

1 Roll the dough on a lightly floured work surface to a thickness of 6 mm (¼ in). Carefully lift up the dough with the rolling pin and place it into the bowl, avoiding stretching which could cause the dough to split during cooking. Either form a twisted rope edge from 6 mm (¼ in) thick sausages of dough (see page 11) or make ivy leaves using the cutter or template and place them around the edge.

VARIATIONS

See the gift ideas gallery on pages 64-5 for other jewellery ideas and design dishes to match.

2 Make the grapes from dozens of tiny balls of dough. Add a few drops of water to them in your hand and carefully 'pour' them in place, avoiding getting any water on the dish which will stain during cooking. Add grape leaves, making them with the cutter or template, and a twig stalk.

3 Make the earrings by cutting out two leaves for each one and place them on greaseproof paper, overlapping in opposite directions. Make lots of small grapes and pile them on top of the leaves using water, as described in Step 2. It is a good idea to make spares at this stage as they are quick to make and fairly fragile. The brooch was formed by starting with a sausage of dough which the leaves were placed on.

4 Bake immediately at about 80 °C (175 °F) (fan oven) or 100 °C (210 °F) (convection oven) for 4-6 hours, or gas mark ¼ for 2-3 hours, or until solid (see page 17). Then paint (see page 18). I painted the leaves with a light wash of sap green tinged with brown, and the grapes are brilliant violet mixed with Payne's grey.

5 Once the paint has dried, glue the appropriate findings onto the back of the pieces of jewellery using the two-part epoxy resin or hot glue. Metal does not stick well to varnish so glue on the findings prior to varnishing. When varnishing, take care that you don't get a pool in the bottom of the trinket dish.

BASKETS AND BOWLS GALLERY

Woven wheat-edged basket

Strips of dough have been woven together and baked in a glass pie dish. A potato ricer was then used for the wheat stalks and the ears of wheat snipped using scissors.

Cluster of fruits-edged bowl

Made with a lattice pie cutter, the twisted rope then encircles three-quarters of the edge and the leaves and flowers — highlighted with watercolours — nestle in the gap.

Natural dough, nut and fir cone dish

A twisted rope curls around the top of this dish (made with a pie cutter) decorated with fir cones, nuts and dough fruits. This is a good one to start with as it is quick to make.

Greek key bowl

To make the regular key pattern around the edge of this bowl, I pressed a length of shiny cord into the dough. To finish it off, the top is made from a simply twisted rope.

Dough fruits cooked in a wicker basket

This basket has been lined with a dough cloth, filled with scrunched-up foil, and then covered with dough fruits. Make sure you use a wicker basket which has not been varnished as it will fume when cooking.

Star-edged dish

Stars and holly leaves were attached to the edge of this simply made bowl. Unfortunately, water got on the base during this process so it is not too beautiful — hence the doily. The stars are painted with a lovely gold gouache.

GARLANDS AND WREATHS

You can really go to town with garlands and wreaths as dough can be made up in several pieces and either joined later, or hung together. The swag and tails featured opposite can be made even more dramatic by joining the tails closely to the swag on either side. If you intend to make a large project, give yourself plenty of time as it is best to complete it the day you start.

PRIMROSE AND APPLE BLOSSOM GARLAND

Capture spring with this delicate coloured swag of trailing ivy and flowers. It would look very pretty hanging above a dresser or sideboard. If you do not have a large enough baking tray for this project, make it up in three pieces and stick them together before painting.

1 Roll out half the dough into a thick sausage about 84 cm (33 in) long. Roll it slightly to flatten to 4 cm (1½ in) wide and then place on the baking tray. Cut out the primrose and apple leaves either by cutting around a few different sized fresh ones or use the templates on page 78. Vein the leaves (see page 16) and place them on the garland overlapping the edges. Make plenty so that the garland is nearly covered at this stage.

YOU WILL NEED

2 batches of dough (page 8)
Rolling pin
Large baking tray, lightly greased
Knife
Container of water
Fresh primrose and apple leaves or templates (page 78)
Blossom cutters or templates, 2.5 cm (1 in) and 12 mm (½ in) diameters (page 78)
Pointed tool or pencil
Primrose cutter or template (page 78)
Star pointed modelling tool
Ivy leaf cutters or templates (page 78)
Paints (page 18)
Paintbrushes
Varnish (pages 18-19)
Drill, glue and wire for hanging

VARIATIONS

Why not make a matching trinket dish for a dresser? Holly and Christmas roses would make a very festive variation.

2 Cut out apple blossoms using the 2.5 cm (1 in) blossom cutter or template, and press in place with the pointed tool or pencil. Similarly, cut out primroses using the cutter or template, and press into position with the star pointed tool.

3 To make apple blossom buds, use the small blossom cutter to make the calyx and mould it over a pea-sized ball of dough. Make plenty of these and place in little clusters along the garland. Thinly roll sausages of dough for the trailing ivy and then cut out three sizes of ivy leaf graduating the sizes from large to small.

4 To form rosettes, roll a sausage of dough to 25 cm (10 in) long and flatten to 4 cm (1½ in) wide. Wet along one edge, pleat into a circle and attach to the top left corner of the garland. Repeat for the top right corner of the garland.

5 Bake immediately at about 80 °C (175 °F) (fan oven) or 100 °C (210 °F) (convection oven) for 18-24 hours, or gas mark ¼ for 9-12 hours, or until solid (see page 17). Then paint and varnish (see pages 18-19). I painted the apple blossom with permanent rose gouache paint tinged with white towards the edges, the leaves are sap green, the ivy Hooker's green, and the primroses are cadmium yellow with a touch of yellow ochre in their centres. Drill and glue in wires on both sides for hanging (see page 19).

TWISTED AUTUMN GARLAND

Why not capture an autumn walk on this colourful garland? Hunt for beech nut shells and real acorns, or make dough acorns as I have. Substitute little fir cones for the nuts if you wish. This garland would look equally good if left unpainted.

1 Take two-thirds of the dough and roll into two long, thick sausages. Lay one sausage over the other, twist into a rope (see page 11) and then make into a circle with a diameter of 23 cm (9 in) on the baking tray. Make the join at the bottom where it will not be seen. Finally, flatten 10 cm (4 in) along the bottom.

YOU WILL NEED

1 batch of dough (page 8)
Rolling pin
Baking tray, lightly greased
Container of water
Sharp knife
Leaf cutter or template (page 78)
Pointed modelling tool or old pencil
A few twigs
Beech nuts
Hazel nuts
Almonds
Acorn leaf cutter or template (page 78)
Drinking straw
Ribbon or drill, glue and wire for hanging
Paints (page 18)
Paintbrushes
Varnish (pages 18-19)

VARIATIONS

This garland can be adapted for any season. Make lilac for early summer, or masses of roses and sprigs of lavender. For Easter, how about primroses and little decorated eggs? Holly, Christmas roses, fir cones and tangerines tied with a rich red satin ribbon would make a perfect present.

2 Cut some leaves either freehand or using the leaf cutter or template. Fix in place along the bottom of the ring and then make three apples (see page 12) and position on top of the leaves. Make five blackberries (see page 12) and four or five acorns (see page 14) and also push into position.

3 Fill gaps with beech nut shells, hazel nuts and almonds. Then add a few small oak leaves using the cutter or template to make them before positioning over the nuts.

4 If you want to hang the garland with ribbon, core out two holes with the drinking straw. If you prefer to hang it invisibly, drill and add wire after the wreath has been baked (see page 19).

5 Bake immediately at about 80 °C (175 °F) (fan oven) or 100 °C (210 °F) (convection oven) for 18-24 hours, or gas mark ¼ for 9-12 hours, or until solid (see page 17). Then paint and varnish (see pages 18-19). I painted the leaves with sap green tinged with brown, the blackberries are a mixture of alizarin crimson and Payne's grey, and the apples ochre and orange, finished off with a dry brush of alizarin crimson.

NATURAL DOUGH WREATH

This is the perfect project to begin with as no painting is needed. This large wreath is made from two batches of dough, but you can make it any size you want depending on baking trays available. Use the technique as a starting point and vary the fruits as you wish. The little wreath on page 46 is formed in the same way but has been decorated with blossoms, acorns and oak leaves.

1 Roll a long sausage with about a third of the dough and form it into the required sized circle on your baking sheet. This one is 30 cm (12 in) in diameter. Join the dough. Then roll some dough from each of the plain, buckwheat and rye doughs into sheets about 6 mm (¼ in) thick and cut a large selection of leaves from them either freehand or by using the cutters or templates. Lay these on the wreath, overlapping the inner and outer edges.

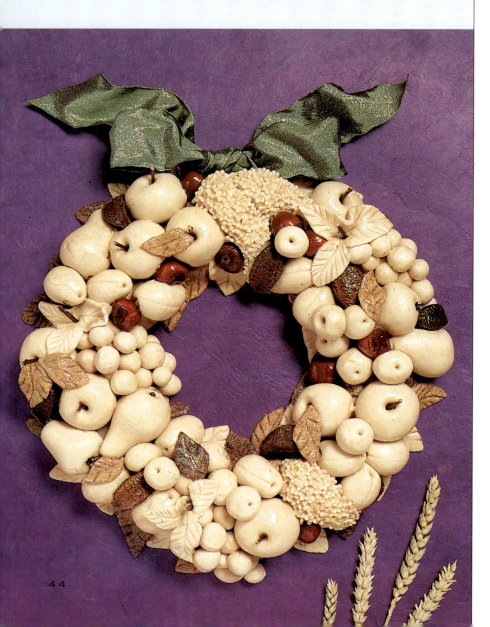

— VARIATIONS —

This wreath will look completely different if you choose to paint it in rich, vibrant colours. Alternatively, give it a wash with beaten egg for a darker colour without having to bake at a high temperature. But be warned: you cannot paint over egg wash once it is cooked.

2 Make three bunches of grapes (see page 12) and drape them around the wreath. Then make some apples, pears and plums (see pages 12-13) and place them on the wreath in groups. Top them off with some cherries made by rolling small balls of dough and indenting the tops with an old pencil.

3 Make the trails of blossoms by starting with cones of dough and covering them with tiny blossoms either using the ejector cutter or by pushing the blunt end of the paintbrush in to make them stand up.

4 Wet the nuts and push them in to the wreath to fill any gaps. This is a good way of using up old nuts left over from Christmas. Finally, add a few more leaves on top.

5 Bake immediately at about 100 °C (175 °F) (fan oven) or 120 °C (210 °F) (convection oven) for up to 24-36 hours, or at Gas mark ¼ for 12-24 hours, or until solid (see page 17). This is a very thick wreath and will take a long time to cook. Once the wreath is baked you may like to turn the oven up by about 40 °C (100 °F) for 10-15 minutes in order to brown it. Turn off the oven and leave to cool down slowly. Varnish with two coats. Drill and glue in wire for hanging (see page 19).

GARLANDS AND WREATHS GALLERY

Natural dough garland

This was made in the same way as the natural dough wreath on page 44, using a small quantity of left-over dough.

Buckwheat, rye and plain flour wreath

These delightful mice nestling in their flowerpots were made from a mixture of doughs and the pots were half filled with aluminium foil to speed the baking process.

Fruited swag

This magnificent wall hanging was
made using three batches of
dough. The base is covered
with leaves, fruit and
flowers so that none of
it shows through.

Ribbons and cherries

This colourful garland was quickly made
from about half a batch of dough.

MIRRORS AND FRAMES

*H*ere is a useful way of using dough and as long as it is hung in a warm, dry atmosphere, it will come to no harm. A framed photograph makes a very personal present and mirrors are a useful addition to any home. Mirrors and glass can both be cut using a good quality tile cutter but make sure that you wear stout gloves when handling, and goggles to protect your eyes from splinters of glass. I tend to use clip frames for extra safety as the frame itself hangs on the wall and the dough is glued on afterwards.

SUNFLOWER FRAME

Let the sunshine in with this summery sunflower picture frame which will brighten any wall. If the thought of making so many flowers puts you off, why not make one large one at the top and cover the rest in leaves? For extra safety, a purchased clip frame has been used — make sure it is glass and not plastic at the front.

1 Lay the clip frame on the baking tray with the glass still in place, cut a strip of corrugated cardboard long enough to fit all the way around and cover it with a doubled piece of folded, lightly greased aluminium foil. This will help give a little padding and allow the dough to expand slightly without cracking during baking. Roll out dough to form a flattened sausage 4 cm (1½ in) wide. Cut two pieces 23 cm (9 in) long and two pieces 18.5 cm (7¼ in) long. Mitre the corners and lay on the foil — the dough should overlap the edge of the frame by about 12 mm (½ in).

YOU WILL NEED

Clip-style picture frame 18 x 13 cm (7 x 5 in)

Baking tray

Corrugated cardboard

Scissors

Aluminium foil, slightly greased

1 batch of dough (page 8)

Rolling pin

Ruler

Knife

Container of water

Leaf cutter or template (page 78)

Star pointed tool or cocktail stick (toothpick)

Circular cutter, 7 cm (2¾ in) diameter

Paints (page 18)

Paintbrushes

Varnish (pages 18-19)

Silicone sealant

— VARIATIONS —

If you want a more rounded effect on the frame, roll one long sausage of dough to fit all the way around rather than making flattened sausages.

2 Cut out dozens of leaves freehand or use the cutters or templates, making two or three different sizes. Mark veins on them and then position all the way around the frame.

3 Make marble-sized balls of dough and flatten them to form the centre of each flower. Position on the frame and then mark seed effects using the star pointed tool or cocktail stick (toothpick).

4 Cut out sunflower petals using the circular cutter. Make elliptical shapes 3 cm (1¼ in) long and 6 mm (¼ in) wide (see page 16). Place a double layer of petals on each flower.

• Tip: If you are using this to frame a mirror, lay the unpainted frame onto the mirror to see if any overlapping leaves need to be painted underneath. It is too late once it is glued on!

5 Bake immediately at about 80 °C (175 °F) (fan oven) or 100 °C (210 °F) (convection oven) for 12 hours, or gas mark ¼ for 6 hours. Then remove the dough from the clip frame, lay on a baking rack, and return to the oven for a further 6 hours (electric) or 3 hours (gas), or until solid (see page 17). Then paint and varnish (see pages 18-19) avoiding the area to be glued onto the frame. I painted the leaves sap green, the flowers cadmium yellow darkened with ochre and the centres brown. Use silicone sealant to attach the dough to the clip frame, but remember to put your picture into it first.

SHELL MIRROR

This Shaker-style frame will look good in any warm, dry bathroom. I have made it from a mixture of shells, some found on a shell beach on holiday, and some purchased. I fell in love with the glass nuggets and just had to include them. Look out for green or blue nuggets which might look even better. The mirror can be hung using rope or sisal, or drill and stick on a wire hook if you prefer (see page 19).

1 Make a cardboard template 20.5 cm (8¼ in) square with an aperture of 9 cm (3½ in). Roll some of the dough to a thickness of 8 mm (⅜ in). Mark the hanging holes 2.5 cm (1 in) in from the edges using the cocktail stick (toothpick). Lay the template over the rolled dough and cut around the frame and aperture with the craft knife. Smooth the edges and core out the hanging holes using the drinking straw.

YOU WILL NEED

Cardboard
Scissors
1 batch of dough (page 8)
Rolling pin
Baking tray, lightly greased
Craft knife
Cocktail stick (toothpick)
Pencil
Large drinking straw
Container of water
Garlic press
Seaweed templates (page 78)
Knife
Shells
Glass nuggets
Craft glue
Varnish (pages 18-19)
Paintbrush
Mirror
Silicone sealant
Felt and card for backing (optional)
Sisal rope or raffia for hanging

2 Use the garlic press to form seaweed arranged in little clumps around the frame, and then cut some larger pieces of seaweed fronds either freehand or using the template.

3 Press shells into the dough, scattering them around the frame. Also add little clusters of nuggets in either one, or a selection of colours.

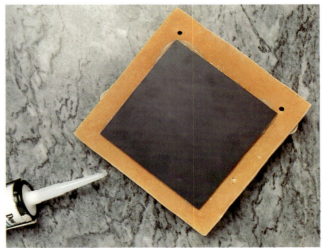

4 Bake immediately at about 80 °C (175 °F) (fan oven) or 100 °C (210 °F) (convection oven) for 8-12 hours, or at Gas mark ¼ for 4-6 hours, or until solid (see page 17). The glass nuggets will stubbornly refuse to stick to the dough once it is cooked, so they will need to be stuck in place with craft glue at this stage. Paint if you wish, and then varnish (see pages 18-19). I used some Hooker's green and then a wash of gold gouache on the shells. If you use matt varnish, you may prefer not to get any on the nuggets as it dulls them.

5 Glue the mirror to the back of the frame using silicone sealant, or some other suitable glue, and cover if you wish with felt-covered card. Thread sisal, rope or raffia through the hanging holes and adjust to the required length.

VARIATIONS

Why not tie up bundles of soaps with matching rope or raffia decorated with shells? Likewise, glass jars filled with shells and pebbles always look pretty. If you use shells you have collected, why not put a holiday snapshot in the frame instead of the mirror?

CHAMPION PICTURE FRAME

A framed photograph makes a lovely personalised gift and this frame, symbolising success, would be equally suitable for a sports day photograph or any other sporting event. Vary the size to suit your photograph.

1 Draw a circle on some silicone paper the size needed to fit your picture plus 2.5 cm (1 in), cut it out and place on the baking tray. Take enough dough to form a sausage of dough to fit around the circle, roll out and lay around the marked circle. Cut and dampen the ends to form a ring and then flatten slightly.

YOU WILL NEED

Silicone paper
Baking tray, lightly greased
½ batch of dough (or more for a larger frame) (page 8)
Knife
Circular cutter
Rolling pin
Stub wire
Wire cutters
Paints (page 18)
Varnish (pages 18-19)
Cardboard
Felt
Craft glue

—— VARIATIONS ——

Try trailing ivy or cascading grapes or lilac for a change, or substitute holly and red berries for a Christmas frame.

2 Using the circular cutter, make the laurel leaves (see page 16), vein them with the back of the knife and put in place around the ring. Make a few balls of dough for berries and add them, too.

3 To make the ribbon effect, roll out a strip of dough to 2 mm (¹⁄₁₀ in) thick and about 3.6 mm (1½ in) wide and pleat. You could use coloured dough for the ribbon if you prefer.

4 Dampen, cut to size and press gently into position. For hanging the frame, push a folded piece of stub wire into the top (or drill and glue later if making a large frame, see page 19).

5 Bake immediately at about 80 °C (175 °F) (fan oven) or 100 °C (210 °F) (convection oven) for 10-12 hours, or at Gas mark ¼ for 5-6 hours, or until solid (see page 17). Then paint and varnish (see pages 18-19). I painted the leaves with sap green, the ribbons with alizarin crimson, and the berries with yellow and red mixed to make a good bright orange. To finish off, stick your chosen photograph in place and back the whole by cutting a circle of card 3.6 cm (1½ in) smaller than the frame. Cover with felt or fabric and glue onto the back of the frame to cover the photograph.

MIRRORS AND FRAMES GALLERY

Seashore walk mirror

This pretty frame is made of a collection of driftwood, glass, shells, dried seaweed and stones. The mermaid, rusty anchor, and treasure chest add a little fantasy.

Grape and fig mirror

This mirror started life as a disaster as it was an early effort at framing a mirror and the dough broke in two during baking. I salvaged it and think that the silver gouache added to the paints gives a lustrous finish.

Heart frame

I used a large heart-shaped cutter to make this frame which would be delightful scaled down as a tree decoration.

Trellis frame

Wild strawberries and ivy combine to make this frame. The outline was drawn on silicone paper and the dough cut to size.

GIFT IDEAS

Salt dough is an ideal medium for making all manner of gifts and apart from time, the cost is minimal. Use the ideas in this section as a launch pad for your own models, changing and adapting them depending on the recipient's interests. In addition to the pig clock and teddy book ends, there are yet more ideas in the gallery on pages 64-5.

PIG CLOCK - EXERCISE TIME

Here is a challenging way to use dough. Either buy a clock movement (see page 79) or recycle one from a clock you have grown tired of. Before you start, make sure that you will be able to fit the clock movement through the dough.

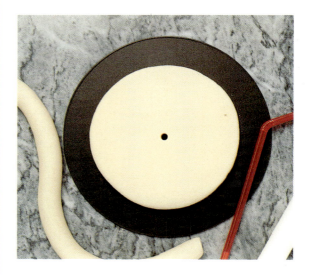

1 Roll a circle of dough that is 6 mm (¼ in) thick and has a diameter of 17 cm (6½ in) and lay it on the baking tray. Cut out the centre using the drinking straw making sure that this hole is large enough to fit the clock mechanism through, remembering that dough shrinks slightly during baking. Make a rope of dough (see page 11) long enough to fit all the way around the clock. Cut and join it neatly at what will be the bottom of the clock, avoiding stretching the dough as you work.

YOU WILL NEED

Clock movement at least 6 mm (¼ in) thick
1 batch of dough (page 8)
Rolling pin
Baking tray, lightly greased
Large drinking straw
Container of water
Knife
Pointed tool
Cocktail sticks (toothpicks)
Paints (page 18)
Paintbrush
Varnish (pages 18-19)
Drill, glue and wire for hanging

—— **VARIATIONS** ——

To make a clock for a child's bedroom replace the pigs with teddy bears – see the book end bears on pages 62-3 for making.

2 Make the pig parts from equal quantities of dough, making little balls for their bodies with indentations for the arms, legs and heads. Cut arms and legs to the same length, and mark trotters with the back of a knife.

3 Position the bodies, arms, legs and heads on the clock face, each in a different pose. Make faces by rolling tiny balls of dough for the snouts and pressing in the pointed tool to make the nostrils. Indent eyes if you wish or leave them at this stage and paint them in later. Then add the ears.

4 Make leg warmers and towel from thinly rolled dough. Pleat it for the leg warmers and cut a fringe in the ends of the towel. Make dumbbells from a short length of cocktail stick (toothpick) with a tiny ball of dough on each end, and make the skipping rope from a thin rope of dough attached to handles.

5 Carefully lay the exercise pieces in place. Use a cocktail stick (toothpick) to help position the leg warmers around the legs and place the towel over the join in the rope edging. Bake immediately at about 80 °C (175 °F) (fan oven) or 100 °C (210 °F) (convection oven) for 12-18 hours, or at Gas mark ¼ for 6-9 hours, or until solid (see page 17). Then paint and varnish (see pages 18-19). I used magnolia emulsion to paint the background, and then white gouache tinted with a little permanent rose for the pigs. I then mixed white to intense blue to make a pale blue for the leg warmers, and finally painted silver gouache for the dumbbells. Then fit the clock movement, gluing it in place. Drill and glue in wire for hanging (see page 19).

TEDDY BEAR BOOK ENDS

The weight of salt dough makes it ideal for these delightful book ends. Make the supports from an extra batch of dough if you are not able to make the wooden bases and allow plenty of time for baking. This project requires some patience but it will be well rewarded. They could be personalized for a child by writing the titles of their favourite stories on the covers of the books. The possibilities are endless!

1 Start by making the bookends. Sand the edges of the wood, round off the corners and then glue the shorter piece of wood to the longer pieces. Hammer in two panel pins for extra strength and once the glue is dry, carefully fill the nail holes with filler. Finish off with the varnish or the coloured satin wood stain.

YOU WILL NEED

2 pieces of wood 13 x 9 cm (5¼ x 3½ in)
2 pieces of wood 14.5 x 9 cm (5¾ x 3½ in)
Sandpaper
Wood glue
Hammer
4 panel pins
Wood filler
Varnish or satin wood stain
For the teddies
1 batch of dough (page 8)
Rolling pin
Knife
Container of water
Peppercorns
Cocktail stick (toothpick)
Deep square or oblong cake tin, lined and lightly greased
Paints (page 18)
Paintbrushes
Varnish (pages 18-19)
Craft glue

VARIATIONS

Let your imagination run wild — how about replacing the teddies with keep-fit pigs, sleeping cats, or sheep sitting knitting.

2 Now make the teddies by forming a body shape with indentations for the legs and arms. Make the arms by rolling enough dough for four and cutting into four equal sized pieces for both teddies. This helps to ensure all the arms are the same size. Repeat for the legs, turning up the ends to make feet.

3 Make the heads from balls of dough. Make indentations for the eyes and press in peppercorns. Mark noses and mouths using the knife and stick on their ears. Texturize the teddies with the cocktail stick — it will feel like it takes forever (see page 10 for alternative methods of adding texture).

4 Piece together the teddies on the lined and lightly greased cake tin and then make their accessories. Make a stack of little books and one open book from thinly rolled dough, marking the pages with a knife. Give one teddy a bow tie cut from rolled dough. Make a hot water bottle and mark it with a criss-cross pattern.

5 Bake immediately at a 45-degree angle to preserve the shapes. One of my bears sagged a little in the oven but it has given him extra character. He looks very relaxed! Bake at about 80 °C (175 °F) (fan oven) or 100 °C (210 °F) (convection oven) for 18-24 hours, or at Gas mark ¼ for 9-12 hours, or until solid (see page 17). Then paint and varnish (see pages 18-19). I used a light wash of Vandyke brown for the bears and primary colours for the books. Finally, glue the teddies and books into place using a craft glue.

SAFETY NOTE
Remember that this is not a toy and is not suitable to be given to very young children.

GIFT IDEAS GALLERY

Napkin rings

These are easy to make to match candle holders or centrepieces (see page 11).

Paperweights

Unless you particularly want an extremely heavy paperweight, make it with a small ball of aluminium foil in the centre to allow it to bake more quickly. Stick a piece of felt on the bottom to protect furniture.

Badges and earrings

Badges, brooches and earrings can be made in almost any design but remember to make a left and right design for each pair of earrings.

Gift tag and decoration ideas

Make your own gift tags from scraps of leftover dough. Make a tiny hole for threading ribbon through before you bake them and paint or write your message on the dough before varnishing.

Light or blind pull

Take a piece of cord long enough for your project, tie a bead or button to the end of it and work the dough around it. Then suspend in the oven and bake at a very low temperature so that the cord does not melt.

Pig in a parachute lampshade

This pig weighs a ton — to lighten the load incorporate a ball of foil in his tummy.

Dominoes

Peppercorns were used instead of paint to mark the dots on these dominoes. Alternatively, indent the numbers with a flat-headed nail dipped in paint: it will save on painting later.

FESTIVE DECORATIONS

Christmas is my favourite time of year and I could have written a whole book on this section. An advent calendar (see opposite) is a good way of counting down the days to Christmas and children will love hanging a different novelty on the tree each day. If you start early enough, you could make all your gifts for family and friends and also decorate your house for next-to-nothing. Children will love to help make decorations for the tree and for their friends, too.

TREE DECORATIONS

There are many decorations that you can make for your tree but I have chosen just a few to give detailed instructions for making them. Start well before Christmas because the painting and varnishing are quite time-consuming and there are far too many other things to be thinking of at Christmas. Alternatively, have a Scandinavian theme for your tree and either leave the dough its natural colour or use coloured dough.
The choice is yours.

CANDY CANE

This is a very simple and effective decoration to make. To save a lot of time, use coloured dough instead of painting when finished.

1 Roll a small quantity of dough into a thin, even sausage about 15 cm (6 in) long and do the same with a little red dough. Then form the two pieces of dough into a twisted rope (see page 11).

2 Push a paper clip or wire hook into the top of the cane — unless you intend to hang it directly over the branch of the tree. Cut out three holly leaves from green dough and roll a few red berries. Use them to cover the hook. Finally, bake immediately at about 80 °C (175 °F) (fan oven) or 100 °C (210 °F) (convection oven) for 6-8 hours, or at Gas mark ¼ for 3-4 hours, or until solid, and then varnish (see pages 18-19).

CHRISTMAS SHEEP

1 Roll a little dough into sausages to make two legs, each about 5 cm (2 in) long and mark the hooves with the back of a knife. Make the body from an oval blob of dough and place on top of a baking tray.

2 Now for the fun! Using the garlic press, push out 2.5 cm (1 in) lengths of dough and use this to cover the body starting from the outside and working in.

3 Make a head from a small ball of dough and indent the eye sockets using the pointed tool or pencil. Push in wet peppercorns. Form tiny ears from squashed, rolled dough, folded at one end and then placed behind the head. Add horns too if you want.

4 Cut out holly and roll berries from coloured dough and put in place. Push a piece of wire or a paper clip in for hanging. Then bake immediately at about 80 °C (175 °F) (fan oven) or 100 °C (210 °F) (convection oven) for 8-12 hours, or at Gas mark ¼ for 4-6 hours, or until solid, and then varnish (see pages 18-19).

HEART-SHAPED DECORATIONS

These are quick to make using biscuit cutters or a template (see page 78).

1 Roll out the dough to 6 mm (¼ in) thick and cut out heart shapes using the large cutter or template. Place onto a baking tray. Either make a little hole in the top for hanging, or push in a piece of wire or paper clip.

2 Cut and vein leaves (see page 16) and lay in place. Add Christmas roses by cutting out five petals with the briar rose cutter or template and overlap them to make a circle. Push into position using the pointed tool.

3 Finally, fill the centres with a few strands of garlic-pressed dough formed into a point. Bake immediately at 80 °C (175 °F) (fan oven) or 100 °C (210 °F) (convection oven) for 6-8 hours or at Gas mark ¼ for 3-4 hours, or until solid. Then paint and varnish (see pages 18-19). I painted the stamens and around the edge of the heart with a little gold gouache and the leaves are painted with diluted sap green mixed with brown.

TWISTED GARLANDS WITH HANGING STAR OR HEART

These charming little garlands are simpler to make than they look!

1 Make a twisted rope with either plain or coloured dough, or both, and join into a circle about 7.5 cm (3 in) in diameter. Lay on a baking tray. Push a 5 cm (2 in) length of wire through the top of the garland and cover the join with holly and berries made from coloured dough. Cut out a small heart or star shape using the cutters or templates and push a 2.5 cm (1 in) length of wire into it.

2 Bake immediately at about 80 °C (175 °F) (fan oven) or 100 °C (210 °F) (convection oven) for 6-8 hours, or at Gas mark ¼ for 3-4 hours, or until solid (see page 17). Then paint and varnish (see pages18-19). If you haven't used coloured dough, paint the heart with red gouache paint for a dense colour and the star with gold. Using pliers and wire cutters link the holly and berries to the dough, and then the heart or star. Bend and cut the wires to the correct length so that the heart or star hangs centrally in the garland.

SCANDINAVIAN TROLL IN A STOCKING

This christmas decoration has been made with natural dough and painted with gouache paints after baking.

1 Make a cone-shaped body with a small amount of dough (use the template on page 77 as a guide for the body's proportions) and make indentations for the arms and head. Make the troll's head from a ball of dough and add a tiny ball for her nose. Add eyes by making indents with the pointed tool and then roll a sausage of dough for her arms, cut in half at an angle and lay in place.

3 Make the frill also from the template, then for the fur edging, cut some very short pieces of garlic-pressed dough and position the fur carefully right along the top of the stocking.

2 Insert peppercorns into the eye sockets. Using the template, cut out a little dress from dough rolled to a thickness of 6 mm (¼ in) and stick in place. Repeat with the stocking shape.

4 Again using the garlic press, make some long hair and curl it slightly as you position it. Cut out her hat using the template on page 77 and put in place. Now either push in a wire for hanging or drill and glue one in place later (see page 19). Bake immediately at 80 °C (175 °F) (fan oven) or 100 °C (210 °F) (convection oven) for 8-12 hours or at Gas mark ¼ for 4-6 hours, or until solid (see page 17). Then paint and varnish (see pages 18-19). I painted the troll with rich Mars red gouache. The gold stars were also painted with gouache. Vandyke brown was used for her hair and a very pale wash of yellow ochre for her face. Her cheeks were given a gentle pink tint.

CHRISTMAS CANDLE HOLDER

There is something really special about candlelight at Christmas and these candle holders are very simple to make. They can be decorated to coordinate with your table linen, or to fit in with any other celebration such as Thanksgiving or Easter. Make matching napkin rings too (see page 11).

1 Roll some dough to a thickness of 6 mm (¼ in) and cut out a circle of 12 cm (4½ in) diameter. Place on the lightly greased baking tray. Cut a second circle 10-15 mm (½-¾ in) larger than the diameter of your candle and lay it either in the centre of the larger circle or slightly off-centre depending on your choice of design. Push the candle into the smaller circle of dough and mould the edges up around the candle. As the dough contracts during baking, move the candle around slightly to make the hole larger. Remove the candle.

YOU WILL NEED

½ batch of dough (page 8)
Rolling pin
Baking tray, lightly greased
Circular cutters, 12 cm (4 ½ in), and 12 mm (½ in) larger than the candle
Container of water
Candle
Leaf cutter or template (page 78)
Calyx cutter or template (page 78)
Cocktail stick (toothpick)
Paints (page 18)
Paintbrushes
Varnish (pages 18-19)
Felt
Craft glue

2 Using the leaf cutter or template prepare as many leaves as are needed to cover the base (about 20). Vein them (see page 16) and position all over the base varying their angles and pinching some slightly to make the leaves look as realistic as possible.

3 Make poinsettias by cutting out ten petals for each flower, or use the calyx cutter or template. Cut out two sets for each flower and then position one on top of the other. Make the centres of each flower from a small cluster of tiny balls of dough, or one small ball textured with the cocktail stick (toothpick). Then add some Christmas roses (see page 70).

4 Bake immediately at about 80 °C (175 °F) (fan oven) or 100 °C (210 °F) (convection oven) for 8-12 hours, or at Gas mark ¼ for 4-6 hours, or until solid (see page 17). Then paint and varnish (see pages 18-19). I painted the leaves with Hooker's green tinged with brown, the poinsettias with alizarin crimson for the petals and cadmium yellow in the centres, and gold gouache for the rose centres.

5 Glue a circle of felt on the bottom to protect furniture. When the candle is lit, don't allow it to burn too low, and never leave it unattended.

VARIATIONS

Use any of the ideas from this book to create your unique candle holder designs. Why not make a mass of tiny star-shaped candle holders for a really stunning display?

FESTIVE DECORATIONS GALLERY

Golden garland of Christmas fruits, holly and grapes

The perfect decoration to welcome your guests — as long as it is not hung outside. The garland was made as for the natural dough wreath (see pages 44-5) and a light wash of gold gouache applied before varnishing.

Holly brooch and earrings

This simple jewellery is very quick and easy to make and would sell well at a Christmas bazaar.

Scandinavian trolls

These decorations are modelled in much the same way as the one on page 71.

Christmas pudding fridge magnet

This magnet would be an ideal stocking filler, or it could be scaled down and used as jewellery.

Snowman

This smiling fellow would be just as happy as a brooch or tree decoration instead of a fridge magnet.

Goose plaque

A holiday in America was the inspiration for this snow goose. I first made a cardboard template and the goose was cut from 6 mm (¼ in) thick dough. The holly and berries were added at the end.

Christmas bowl

What could be nicer than receiving this bowl filled with home-made Christmas biscuits or truffles and tied up in cellophane?

75

TEMPLATES

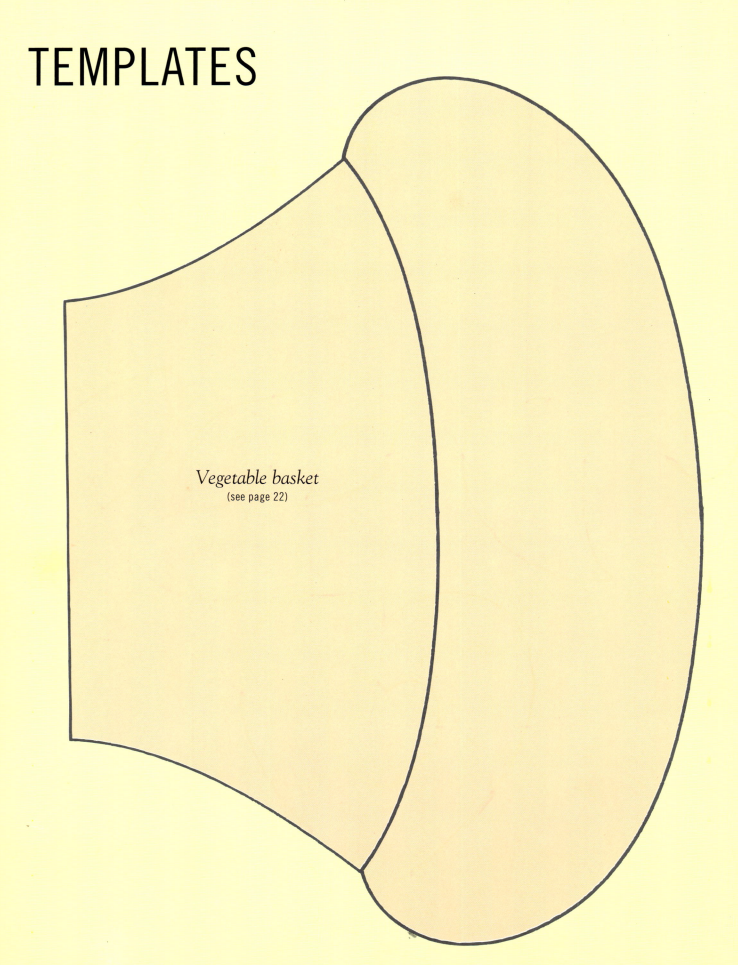

Vegetable basket
(see page 22)

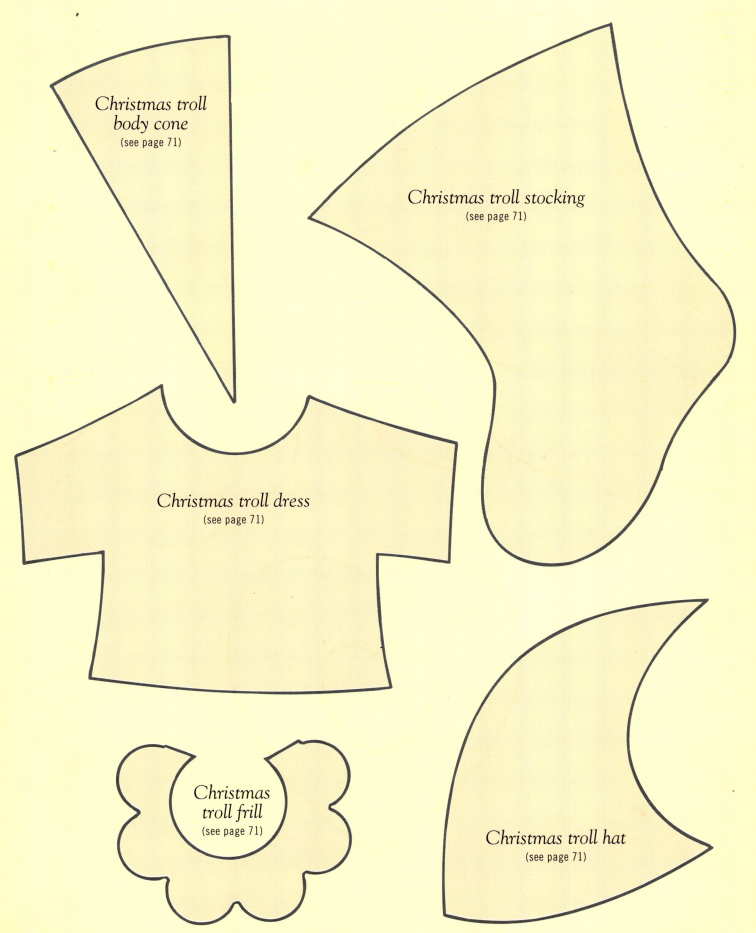

Christmas troll
body cone
(see page 71)

Christmas troll stocking
(see page 71)

Christmas troll dress
(see page 71)

Christmas
troll frill
(see page 71)

Christmas troll hat
(see page 71)

TEMPLATES

Oak
Leaves
(see page 42)

Apple
blossom
(see page 32, 40)

Calyxes
(see page 22, 30, 72)

Ivy
Leaves
(see page 34, 40)

Primrose
(see page 40)

Briar
rose petals
(see page 30, 70)

Leaves
(see page 22, 32,
42, 44, 50,
70, 72)

Natural
dough leaf
(see page 44)

Holly Leaves
(see page 69)

Christmas heart
(see page 70)

Small heart
(see page 70)

Star
(see page 70)

Grape
Leaves
(see page 34)

Seaweed
fronds
(see page 52)

SUPPLIERS

UNITED KINGDOM

Fred Aldous Ltd
PO Box 135
37 Lever Street
Manchester 1
M60 1UX
Tel: (0161) 236 2477
Fax: (0161) 236 6075
(*clock movements, modelling tools, jewellery findings*)

Cake Art Ltd
Venture Way
Crown Estate
Priorswood
Taunton
Somerset TA2 8DE
Tel: (0182) 332 1532
(*general cake decorating supplies*)

Copystat Cardiff Ltd
44 Charles Street
Cardiff CF1 4EE
Tel: (01222) 344422
Fax: (01222) 566136
(*general art suppliers*)

Divertimenti
139-141 Fulham Road
South Kensington
London SW3
Tel: (0171) 581 8065
(*kitchen utensil supplies*)

John Mathieson & Co
48 Frederick Street
Edinburgh EH2 1HG
Tel: (0131) 225 6798
(*general art suppliers*)

Moira Neal
5 Barrowcrofts
Histon
Cambridge CB4 4EU
(*dough making day schools; send SAE*)

J F Renshaw Ltd
Crown Street
Liverpool L8 7RF
Tel: (0151) 706 8200
(*general cake decorating supplies*)

George Rowney & Co Ltd
12 Percy Street
London W1A 9BP
Tel: (0171) 636 8241
(*painting and drawing materials*)

Specialist Crafts Ltd
PO Box 247
Leicester LE1 9QS
Tel: (0116) 251 0405
Fax: (0116) 251 5015
(*mail order*)

Squires Kitchen
Squires House
3 Waverley Lane
Farnham
Surrey GU9 8BB
(*cake icing cutters: send SAE*)

Heffers Art and Graphics
15 King Street
Cambridge
Tel: (01223) 568400
(*painting and drawing materials*)

SOUTH AFRICA

Art Mates
Shop 313
Musgrave Centre
Durban
Tel: (031) 21 0094

Baking Tin
Bloemfontein (051) 481 433
Cape Town (021) 61 6434
East London (0431) 56175
George (0441) 74 6082
Port Elizabeth (041) 334 051
Randburg (011) 792 8189

Corner Arts and Crafts
63 4th Avenue
Newton Park
Port Elizabeth
Tel: (041) 35 2487

The Craftsman
Shop 10
Progress House
110 Bordeaux Drive
Randburg
Tel: (011) 787 1846

Mycrafts Arts and Craft Shop
Aliwal Street
Bloemfontein
Tel: (051) 484 119

Peers Handicrafts
35 Burg Street
Cape Town
Tel: (021) 24 2520

AUSTRALIA

Arts & Crafts Corner
34 Mint Street
East Victoria Park
Western Australia 6101
Tel: (09) 361 4567

Boronia Arts & Crafts Centre
247 Corset Road
Boronia
Victoria 3155
Tel: (03) 762 1751

Cake and Icing Centre
651 Samford Road
Mitchelton
Queensland 4053
Tel: (07) 355 3443

Cake Decorating Centre, The
1 Adelaide Arcade
Adelaide
South Australia 5000
Tel: (03) 223 1719

Finishing Touches Cake
Decorating Centre
268 Centre Road
Bentleigh
Victoria 3204
Tel: (03) 223 1719

Gwen's Timeless Crafts
581 North East Road
Gilles Plains
South Australia 5086
Tel: (08) 369 2243

Hollywood Cake Decorations
52 Beach Street
Kogarah
NSW 2217
Tel: (02) 587 1533

Lincraft
Gallery Level
Imperial Arcade
Pitt Street
Sydney
NSW 2000
Tel: (02) 221 5111

Petersen's Cake Decorations
Rear 698 Beaufort Street
Mt Lawley
West Australia 6050
Tel: (09) 271 1692

Sundale Handcrafts
Shop 11 Logan Hyperdome
Pacific Highway
Loganholme
Queensland 4129
Tel: (07) 810 1121

NEW ZEALAND

Auckland Watch Company
Cnr 102B Albert & Victoria
Streets
Auckland
Tel: (09) 303 4436
(*clock movements*)

Cake Studio, The
3 Mt Eden Road
Mt Eden
Auckland
Tel: (09) 373 3492

Dominion Paint Centre
227 Dominion Road
Mt Eden
Auckland
Tel: (09) 638 7593

Draw Art Supplies Ltd
5 Mahunga Drive
Mangere Bridge
Auckland
Tel: (09) 636 4862

Golden Bridge Marketing Ltd
Cake Decorating Supplies
Cnr Ride Way & William
Pickering Drive
Albany
Tel: (09) 373 3492

INDEX

Page numbers in *italics* represent photographs